T0368335

FOLLOW

the

LEADER

*How to Be a Top Salesperson
by Following God's Lead*

FROSTY RYAN

To order additional copies of this book, contact:
Xlibris
844-714-8691
www.Xlibris.com
Orders@Xlibris.com

ISBN:	Softcover	978-1-6698-7596-3
	EBook	978-1-6698-7595-6

Print information available on the last page

Rev. date: 05/18/2023

CONTENTS

D. How people buy
  1. They buy emotionally
     a. Only hit the areas of where what you have meets what they need
     b. Mirror body language
     c. Control by question
     d. Small Commitments leading to the big one
     e. When "No" means "Yes"
  2. They keep logically
     a. Simple presentation
     b. Beautiful but short proposal: Designed with them in mind
E. Realistic expectations
  1. Then beat them buy under promise and over delivering
  2. Our hearts are in the right place
     a. Not perfect but striving to be there
     b. Issues could be uncovered that were unavoidable but here for you
  3. What makes us different/ original
     a. "Price is only an issue in the absence of value"
F. Assume the deal
  1. Never "So, are you interested" but rather "How would you like it" or "Which do you prefer"
G. Words to avoid
H. Willing to walk away
I. Prepare the referrals and reviews
J. Love the numbers (Law of large numbers)
IV. Sing My Praises?
  A. When and why not
  B. When regrettably I must
V. Know thy Maker
  A. Do I really know Him?
  B. God's loving formula
    1. I pray
    2. He answers

3. I praise
4. He blesses
5. Bible text for each one of them: Proverbs 3:5-6,
C. Pay your tithe and your offerings Proverbs 3:9, 27
D. Always be mastering your craft Proverbs 3:13-18
E. Do not be a yes man to your boss: no one likes it and it will hurt you: Proverbs 3:31-32
F. Keep your head in Heaven while your feet are on the ground: Proverbs 3:35

VI. Balance is beautiful
A. Your health is your wealth
1. Heart healthy: Depression & Anxiety
2. Body healthy: Eating, sleeping, moving
3. Mind healthy: Watch, Hear, See, Speak
4. Spirit healthy: Life with the Creator
B. Down Time
1. Family Time
a. Church: Every week promotes continuity and peace with others
b. Nature: Born of the earth at peace with nature
c. Being together: Daily routines, Monthly meetings, Yearly Landmarks
2. Vacation Time
a. Non-stressful
b. Decompress, Peaceful rest
3. Alone Time
a. Me and God
b. In His word
c. In His Presence
d. Tell it to others

INTRODUCTION

❖

Why this book

I have been in sales for over 30 years now. The reason I am writing this book now is because of 2 major issues. One, I am astonished at how much improvement there still is to be made in the world of helping others get what they want or need. And two, rarely, even close to never do I see salespeople working with The Holy One (God) leading the way. For these reasons it is time to understand that anyone, even those who say, "I just hate sales" can become a master at one of the oldest trades in the world with The Holy One helping you overcome every obstacle.

I graduated from University with a Bachelor's in Religion and a minor in Biblical languages. Don't worry nothing you are about to read will sound like Greek. My wife graduated with a Master's in Business administration. We both graduated then got married the next day and were off on our honeymoon to Disney World. There at Epcot and Disney, we saw something that later would help me understand a clear fundamental rule in sales. That is, being concise. We were amazed at how truly the workers were happy to be working at Disney and to serve our needs. We were also astounded at the cleanliness of everything. They have made that place like "no other on earth." In my sales today I thrive to be original. The original meaning, like no other ordinary salesperson you will encounter. My goal is to make sure that the customers I work for are happy they met me because I made a positive improvement to their existence on this planet while we were here.

After our wonderful honeymoon, we went right into the "Mission Field". Ha ha ha, it's more of a stint since the mission was just north of Nashville, TN. I served as an assistant Chaplin for a boarding academy while my wife Maryon worked in Nashville at an electronics store as a sales rep. After that year of service, I was hired at a large church in Battle Creek, MI as an assistant pastor where my role was to bring back members who had left for whatever reason. We were successful at slowing down the proverbial revolving back door of people who would be baptized and then find themselves leaving within a year. The number one reason people were leaving is they had no friends. The camaraderie was the most powerful reason for someone to stay and continue worshiping at the church so we devised opportunities for long-time church members to fellowship outside of church and become friends with some of the new members. This worked! Later in sales, I learned that the reason many of salespeople leave an organization is that they have not developed a friendship with anyone. You don't have to be "Family" you just need to have someone in your corner who understands the ups and downs and is going through them alongside you.

While working as an assistant pastor I realized that people were never themselves around me. If they knew that I was a pastor they would always apologize for their language (when they cussed) or they would not be honest about their daily lives. I would sometimes certainly hear their heartfelt problems but full honesty as with a friend was lacking. This frustrated me so I found a job as a 10-99 salesperson with a magnificent financial service company and began my road of Die-Hard Sales Training. Years later, I went into another lucrative business of Sales as a project manager with a fast-growing roofing company. The ups and downs were definitely difficult. I do not want you to have to go through every heartache and the stupid mistake you could make in order to learn to become a Master Sales Person. The tools you are about to learn will help you no matter what kind of communication work you are in. Even if you are not in sales, you will learn how to make people like you in less than 90 seconds, how to get along with difficult people, how to have a happier more abundant life than you ever thought possible, and of course how to become one of the top 1 percenters of salespeople in the world all while keeping your Christianity.

Are you ready to explore? Are you ready to discover? I'm so glad you are here and ready for this new adventure. Let's dive in and see how amazing your life will be in the sales world.

One disclaimer: I learned early on as a commissioned salesperson that my whole day was really up to me. When I quickly learned that I was not naturally good at sales I began to work with God. Because I really didn't answer to anyone I learned to depend on God; The big guy, The creator, The head honcho, the main man, the one upstairs, or as we will refer to Him in this book: The Lord.

1
CHAPTER

❖

The Worst Compliment

First, let me explain how I learned that the compliment I'm about to give you, was so bad to receive from a potential customer. After a couple of years in my first sales job I learned all the products to a T. If a potential customer had a question, I was so quick to jump to answer and explain all the ins and outs of the products and services. I would razzle and dazzle them till they had no more questions left and their heads were spinning with all the wonderful information I had to offer about the product was explaining to death, whether they asked about it or not. Then, it would come down to the closing question: "So, would you like to buy." Arg. With this approach, I began to get the same response. "You are a really good salesman." At first, I took that as a nice compliment until noticing that everyone that gave it to me was not signing on the dotted line.

With this knowledge, I began dissecting my approach. 1st I was "throwing up" on my customers. That means giving them way too much information that wasn't even asked for. 2nd I allowed them to control the entire conversation because I was answering all their questions without tossing questions back at them. This was so important. THE TOP SALES PEOPLE CONTROL THE CONVERSATION BY ANSWERING THEIR QUESTION either WITH A QUESTION or answering their question then asking one of their own. Then finally I had to stop sounding like a smooth-talking salesperson by rather finding common ground quickly and talking about other things that were personal to my new friends more than the products I was selling.

1

To summarize this point. DON'T SOUND LIKE A SALESPERSON, SOUND LIKE A HELPFUL FRIEND.

What Doesn't Work

Growing up I would sometimes go with my mom as she haggled with the used car salesman. She knew what she was going to pay and not a dime more. Specifically, on this one occasion, after sitting in the salesman's office with the manager for an hour she finally just got up and left. She told them, "You know how to get ahold of me if you change your mind." We went home. I said, "Mom, don't you want that car?" "Yes," she calmly stated, "But, I'm not paying what they want me to pay for it. You watch I'll get a phone call pretty soon when they decide that my price was fair." About 2 hours later the phone rang. She answered, talked a bit, then hung up with a satisfied smile and we kids looked at her. She said, "See, it's all a game." From that point, I told myself, "I will never be a salesman. "I hate sales." Don't get me wrong, I love playing games, but when it comes down to so much money it just seems like a headache. Later I learned the truth about sales. It's in everything we do; from the begging person on the corner to the child in mom's grocery cart thinking how wonderful it would be to have some of that candy on the shelf, to asking for that special person's hand in marriage, to telling ourselves why this is the right home, church, auto mechanic for me. Our lives are filled with sales. The real problem is with the uncomfortable word itself. It derives for all of us a negative connotation. Therefore, in your mind, you must turn the word into something different whenever you hear it. Turn it into something that it is but that also sounds pleasant. Instead of sales think of getting something needed or wanted. WE ARE NOT SALESPEOPLE BUT RATHER PEOPLE WHO HAVE SOMETHING THAT SOMEONE ELSE NEEDS OR DESIRES. "How may I help you get what you're looking for?"

Beware of words that derive bad emotions. I know you're thinking, "But, I must tell the truth, I must be honest." Yes, you must but you mustn't be a belligerent or a babbling fool. A Police Officer whose buddy was killed in the line to duty doesn't call his buddy's wife and the phone and say, "Hey, sorry, Franks dead. He got shot in the head and now we'll never see him again." No, because that would be one of the rudest things they could do. Instead, the words are carefully and heartfully chosen as to lessen the pain as much as humanly possible. In helping people get what they need we must be a conduit of smooth sailing to the right choice for them. If I'm selling alarm systems door to door and I know this customer needs it and they have the money something I wouldn't say is, "Let me <u>pitch</u> you this idea" or "The other alarm companies are terrible because we are the best of the best." In a few more chapters you'll learn what words to avoid and what words to use. It must be stated right up front that "People buy emotionally and keep logically." It's neurological says Michael Harris in his salesforce journal on May 29, 2015. Once this is understood you are on your way to being a top 1 percenter as a sales master. First, let's find out why most people are just not interested in what you have to sell and how to help them become interested.

Don't Die "Broca"

A little play on words here to help you remember one specific part of the mind that will help you on your wonderful journey in helping people get what they need and get it from YOU! Broca is an area in the frontal lobe hemisphere of the brain that is linked to speech production and speech interception. This area of the brain is the part that tells you that you have seen, heard, smelled, tasted, or done something before. It is the gatekeeper to the rest of the brain that tells you what a situation is all about and helps the rest of your brain determine if this is the same old situation you have already gone through and if it's worth going through it again.

You've heard the old adage, "Been there, done that." That is exactly what Broca tells the rest of your reasoning at the moment something looks familiar. This is the "gatekeeper" of the person seeking your product's brain that you must learn to get past. How, do you get past this clever gatekeeper? By being wise. Wisdom is not just knowledge. It is understanding and responding with ease. Broca knows and can smell a bad, uninteresting salesperson from a long way off. So, you must not be that person. How? Simple. STOP DOING THINGS THAT AVERAGE AND ORDINARY SALESPEOPLE DO AND SAY.

Some examples of what NOT to do or say:

- Come directly at the person in your store with a gleam (dollar signs) in your eye
- The first thing out of your mouth is, "Hello, how is your day." Or "how are you doing?" Whether on the phone or in-person stop saying this immediately. If you don't know someone then you don't really care so it is fake right off the bat. Once you really know them and you really care about them then you can ask them these niceties. In the future.
- Slicking the hair back
- Putting your hand straight out as an aggressive gesture for a firm hand-shake without first feeling they are interested in your presence through strong eye contact
- Telling potential customers how wonderful your company is before knowing what they are really looking for
- "Throwing up" in front of them, meaning telling them all about how something works or all the benefits of the product when they haven't asked
- Jumping right into the sale pitch before getting to know something about the customer first

We, as professional people, must: Be different, walk different, talk different and look different than the normal-looking salesperson if we ever want to get past the gatekeeper of their mind and help them get what they want and need.

I always know immediately when a sales call is coming through because the first words I hear are, "How are you doing today, sir." Already I'm on the defensive. If you are making cold calls you must talk and sound different. Most people are drawn to a baritone or alto style of voice. So, change the tonality of your voice. Yes, you can. Make your voice more melodic and pleasant. Take singing lessons if you need to. Some people will stay on the phone just to talk with you to hear your pleasant voice. Now, with that new voice ask them this question as soon as they answer the phone: "Hey, my name is (first name), and I was wondering something." Then pause and wait for them to ask what it is you are wondering. After that, ask them if (something short and interesting about your product) would be interesting to them. Don't tell the potential customer you are not selling them something if your ultimate goal is to sell them something. Lying only leads to frustration and mistrust and ultimately phone lines dropped.

Regarding in-person sales. Usually, we do not know what a customer is thinking. Until you have studied the looks of a thousand potential interests you will not know enough to guide the conversation in the right direction. For this reason, you must trust The Lord. Send up a quick thought glance to God and ask Him to direct your words so that you can help this potential customer get what they want at an affordable price where everyone wins.

Then begin to study the looks, the responses to your discovery questions, the body language, and the eye shifting. The more you study customers the better you naturally get. Listen to what The Lord is telling you because He's giving you insight. Practice with your coworkers to get better and better. Come to work early and stay late so you will have sales that others are unwilling to work for. DO WHAT OTHERS WON'T SO YOU CAN HAVE WHAT OTHERS DON'T. Never turn down a lead or prospect just because it's too small or you think it's not worth it. Every single potential customer is worth it even if it is just to help you master your craft of salesmanship. Also, as you will learn, there is a law of numbers that when it is embraced you will fall in love with all the yeses AND the nos.

2

CHAPTER

❖

The Master Sales Person

After years of training and thousands upon thousands of meetings with potential buyers, I have learned a secret that most sales managers hate to hear. Here it is. Learn to not care. That's right you must learn to not care about the deal until the deal is done. Let me unpack this statement so it makes total sense. Too many new salespeople "Have to make THIS sale", or "I'm gonna get this one." Before there is any known reason as to  why they should get this one. It reminds me of the 2 times I went to have fun at a casino and the attitude of all the broke customers playing the slots was the same. "This one's gonna be mine baby, I can just feel it." This is an absolute presumption of what the holy scriptures warn us about. We don't know which potential customers will become Bonafede customers until not only have they paid, the commissions are deposited into our account and will not charge back but when that happy customer either gives us a warm referral or leaves a 5-star review online. STOP WISHING, STOP NEEDING, STOP HOPING IN SOMETHING OUT OF DESPERATION. Learn to know that The Lord will take care of you but will only take care of you if you are relying on Him along with doing your part (best efforts). If you depend solely on yourself then you will get only what you are good for. I'd rather get what He wants for me. Wouldn't you?

I've come to the conclusion that the top salespeople in the world have learned to live by a song. It's in their heart even if subconsciously. The song is by one of the best-loved singers of our generation. He sang a few duets with Dolly Parton and several top number 1 hits in the 80s and 90s. This sales song is The gambler song by Kenny Rogers and written by Don Schlitz. Yes, it's a song about life but sales really is in all of our lives and when selling these lyrics make perfect sense. Here let's read the lyrics and you'll understand why. "He said, "Son, I've made a life Out of readin' people's faces Knowin' what the cards were By the way they held their eyes So if you don't mind my sayin' I can see you're out of aces For a taste of your whiskey I'll give you some advice"

[1] So I handed him the bottle And he downed my last swallow Then he took a cigarette And asked me for a light Then the night got deathly quiet And his face lost all expression Said, "If you're gonna play the game, boy You have to learn to play it right

[2] You've have to know when to hold 'em Know when to fold 'em Know when to walk And know when to run You don't count your money When you're sitting at the table There'll be time for counting When the dealings done

[3] Everyone should know the secret to surviving Is knowing what to throw away And knowing what to keep. Every hand's a winner And every hand's a loser And the best that you hope for Is to go in your sleep"

[4] And when he'd finished speakin' He turned back toward the window, Crushed out the cigarette and
Faded off to sleep And somewhere in the darkness, well, The gambler, broke even But in his last words, I found an ace that I could keep

So, the new gambler is talking with the old gambler at his last dying breath and asking him for advice on becoming great. The old gambler takes his last "meal" and begins to tell him the secrets to winning. In **1** the old gambler states, "If you're gonna play the game, …you gotta learn to play it right." This is the same as when scripture tells us in Luke 14:28 that if a person is going to build a tower (Good Life or Business) "Won't you first sit down and estimate the cost to see if you have enough money to complete it." Meaning if you don't have the desire in you for sales now it may never come to you. You must first count the cost; The training, the ups, and downs so that later on when you reach the top of the proverbial mountain you can look back and know it was all worth it.

In chorus **2**, really explains the entire sales process that a master salesperson will learn to have. Firstly, there are so many things about your product/service that if you divulge it all upfront your interested party will become uninterested in a heartbeat. The master will hold back the "Ace" (that one thing that makes your product/service better than anyone else's) until the exact right time. The Lord will tell you when the right time is if you are listening to Him.

Know when to fold 'em. This is important because the folded hand means you know that no matter what you do or say the deal is a bust. If you keep on pushing the sale you will only hurt your reputation and that of the companies. However, if you have a partner at the table (another salesperson) you could politely bow out of the game and pass the deal over to them because they may have more rhythm with the customer to make the deal than you.

Know when to walk away and know when to run: Walking away is because you just do not have what the customer is looking for so there is no way for you to help them this time but being polite will prove to be valuable down the road. When to run: When the customer is very interested, in fact so interested it's too good to be true. And, you know what that means. The customer is either going to use your numbers to bring down the price of your competitor and buy from them anyways or they are simply a terrible customer. That's right. There are terrible customers. The ones that think they are right but do harm to your companies and your reputation. Stay clear from them once you find them out. In fact, RUN from them. Do not do business with them. The Lord will give you hints to know these types of people. They will say key things like, "Last time I bought ____ I was so upset I had to return it and file a BBB report on them" or "I make all the decisions in my house you don't need to talk with my spouse." Some other attitudes of the wrong customer to stay away from are taken from Nextiva.com Oct. 8, 2019. They Want it cheaper even if it hurts the company or if you the salesperson have to give up your commissions for the sale. "They demand more and more of your attention", they say things to point out their lack of complete honesty, "they are abusive" in words or actions to others, and "make unreasonable demands." These things bring forth the spirit of descension and will harm you if you sell to them. You could be the nicest most honest salesperson in the world but God gave everyone the ability to choose how they will act in situations and sometimes even those that say they are believers can lose their "Belief" when spending their money. Buyers' remorse is tougher on some than on most. Those few that it is tough on because there is something wrong with their spirit will do what they have to in order to make the purchase "worth it" to them. Even bringing down the company, if they could. *"KNOW WHEN TO RUN."*

You never count your money when sittin' at the table. The salespeople that are not sales masters yet are always counting on sales and deals that are not even made yet. You can tell who they are because they have the whole list of all the potential customers and know exactly how much they will make when the deal goes through. The gleam in their eye tells you they already have the money in the bank and they are bragging to The bosses, spouses, and coworkers that they have this deal and that deal is coming in. We must stop with this painful process! What happens is the deal does not come through, people stop listening to what you have to say and you lose all respectability. It tells The Lord that you know better than He does and that you can make it on your own without Him.

So, how do we overcome this attitude that all of us have to overcome? You must deliberately stop listening to the bad voice in your head that tells you to count what your commissions will be. Remember the story of King David when he counts his Army in II Samuel 24? When he was counting his army, it was saying that his trust was in manpower not in the power of the almighty. Over and over again The Holy One fought battles alongside of and for him. Now, David steps outside that trust and looks for the power in his own numbers. The Master Salesperson simply puts their head down, outworks everyone while mastering their craft, and allows The Lord to take care of the purse. Never count your money when you're sitting at the deal table because there is time enough for counting when the money is in your account and the satisfied customer is bringing you in warm referrals.

Part 3 of the song states that the gambler (Master Sales Person) knows the secret to survive is "knowing what to throw away and what to keep". These are the leads to say, "No thank you" to or simply not take them on as a client. "What to keep", are the ones to not only do business with but keep on as a repeat customer and as a referral base.

"Every hand's a winner and every hand's a loser." Reiterates the Top Salespeople attitude in not caring until it's a real deal. These top people know the numbers and are never disappointed because A LOSS IS JUST ONE LEAD CLOSER TO A WIN.

"…the best you can hope for is to die in your sleep." In sales, this means that the happiest people are the ones who go out satisfied. They are not troubled because of physical health issues. They are not miserable because of anxiety or depression issues caused by years of personal mental abuse. They are not unhappy because they jumped from one thing to another always looking for the next whale of a sale. The ones who die in their sleep signify the satisfied because they learned the lifelong principles of patience and growth. These are the fondest principles which I hope you take from this book. May your life be full of abundant joy, your health is as strong as you can make it, your love be as complete as the noonday sun and all your sales become as easy as turning on the cooler water for a refreshing drink.

In section 4 the young gambler finally sees with clarity the answer he was looking for all along. Are you beginning to see it now?

Apathy towards the sale is one of the strongest traits you can learn to have. It gives you the upper hand. It shows that you have a backbone and if necessary, you are willing to walk away from the table at any moment. Once you know all about your craft you can then pick when to choose what to tell the lead. What exactly should you tell the lead? Tell them ONLY what they ask for, then, ask a question. The process is simple like riding a bike. The customer asks you to tell them about the product. Because that question is so vague you ask them, "What about ___ are you most interested in learning." This process of question and answer is key to keeping control of the conversation. A constant headache a new salesperson tends to get is to always have their back up against the wall by only answering question after question, thinking that "once I have answered all of their questions they will buy." Ha ha ha, No worries we all have to learn the hard way. If you must answer a question then the way to keep the positive conversation going is to ask a question back to them once you have answered theirs. For example, The customer asks, "How long is the warranty good for?" Your answer is, "It's good for 10 years but there is an additional warranty of 15 or 20 which would you prefer?"

See, YOU NEVER ASK A CUSTOMER IF THEY WANT WHAT YOU HAVE TO OFFER BUT WHAT PART OF YOUR OFFER IS BEST FOR THEM. Not if but when. Not if but how. Not if but how much.

3

CHAPTER

❖

The Hello

Now, let's start from the beginning of the sale and go through the artistry of closing the deal.

Manage the margins: It's always good to have an office manager that sets up appointments or makes some calls for you. This radiates a professional atmosphere that the company is bigger than just you. When the appointments are set by the office manager be sure to put margins in your day. Just like the paper you are reading has margins around the words your day needs space for things that will come up. Although you have an appointment every hour on the hour from 8 am to 5 pm change those appointments earlier and earlier as you work them. Make your 8 O'clock appointment at 7:50 am then if you are done sooner your 9 am can be at 8:30 and so on. Before you know it you are finished by 2 pm unless an appointment takes longer than usual. But, that's why the margins are there. The number one reason to see your customers sooner is that none of the other competitors will. Remember Broca? Here's how to break that barrier of the bad sales processes right away. Be early, and of course under promise and overdeliver. Be what others aren't so that you stay remembered by the potential customer. Also, it's just plain polite. Call and ask them for permission by saying something like, "I am running a little ahead of schedule is it ok if we meet sooner rather than later?" Some make the appointment because that is the only time they are available so absolutely respect that and tell them, "We can of course keep that time if it is best for you." Then just move the next appointment in the earlier spot. Even with these great daily habits, the customer must feel comfortable in your presence.

It floored me at the beginning of my career that people buy from what they are feeling first. That even the first glance or first voice tones of meeting you would tell the potential customer if they were going to buy or brush you aside. The best, very short book, to read on this is "How to make people like you in 90 seconds or less." That is exactly what the book is about and exactly what top salespeople have learned the art of doing. The author, Nicholas Boothman, a former fashion photographer teaches us that getting people to like us enough to do business with us in less than 90 seconds can be easily learned with just a couple of tips. He states that we must establish a rapport by first talking about something they are interested in. Look around the house. Are there animals, classic cars, children, moved in recently. Anything that you may have in common to get them talking about. People will always feel they had a great conversation with you once you have left if you allowed them to do most of the talking and you truly listened and understood their needs. If you are in a walk-in store environment then ask them how long they've been in town or "Have you been to our store before?" Start by talking about them.

Walking up to the door or up to the potential customer: They will most likely see you coming. Are you walking with confidence or cockiness? Are you polite and well-mannered? Are you sure of your product offerings or scared and looking at your shoes? Really, nothing of what you have to share with them matters until they know that they matter to you. I once heard a Sales Master state, "No one cares how much you know until they know how much you care." Are you a caring person in general? Have you learned to have a positive attitude regardless of life circumstances? If you are this type of person learning these few things will come easy if not natural for you. For the rest of us, the second half of this book is for you. We will learn how to have a life full of abundance. "You can learn to have a positive attitude regardless of your circumstances," says Steve Rizzo the funniest motivational business speaker. "WHEN

COMFORTABLE IN YOUR SHOES THE SALES PROCESS CAN BE SOME OF THE MOST FUN YOU WILL EVER HAVE."

Most people, if you are not selling by calling out of the blue, have the money to purchase what you have to offer. Once that hurdle is jumped then all you have to do is get people to like and trust you. I didn't say, "Like OR trust" you. They must both like AND trust you. I may like you enough to go out on the town with you but not trust you to watch my children and vice versa I may trust you enough to have you watch my children but I can't see us going to the movies together. Almost everything we've discussed so far is easy to learn and it comes with practice but this Like and Trust thing is something you must become. To become a person that is both likable and trustworthy comes from building these characteristics in your own life. Ask yourself, "Would I do business with me?" If you answered, "No!" Which of those is it? Do you see yourself as dishonest or do you really just not like yourself? To overcome these bad characteristics, start with small steps. Start being completely honest to yourself and to those that are closest to you. Share your thoughts and emotions out loud. I know it may be tough especially if you come from a family where they just didn't do those things. But remember, you are a child of the Heavenly King and He does those things. He even wants to hear the simplest thoughts of frustration from your lips. He delights in hearing from you the tiniest feelings of joy. When you start to do this with The Lord He opens up your soul to learn the emotions of others and help meet their needs. Like Abraham was; be friends of both God and people. When you see yourself of great worth because Heaven's greatest treasure was paid for you then you begin to understand how valuable you truly are and anyone you have the opportunity of coming into contact with. By utilizing both ears that The Lord gave you, and really listening to others, you will be able to not only hear the potential customer's needs but feel what they feel and only then be able to offer what will meet their need.

4

CHAPTER

❖

What do they want?

What a customer wants is what the point of the sale should really be. It's not how much can I sell them so that my commissions can be bigger and I can win the next amazing trip and be adored by everyone as the king of sales for the month or year. It is about helping those who are searching. It's been stated I believe by Zig Ziglar that "You can have everything in life you want if you will just help other people get what they want." How to know what they want all comes to the point of simply being a good asker of questions. Ask and listen. Do not respond until they have answered. You must wait for their answer or the whole process is lost to your nervousness. One of the greatest Sales Training I had was with Tom Hopkins University. Tom says, "When you ask a question SHUT UP!" Or you will lose the deal because yourself gets in the way.

I believe we all want to be loved by someone, that we all want to have a happy place to live in a nice home and enjoy reliable transportation with a little entertainment once in a while. We also, do not want to have to worry about the future of making the bills or putting food on the table, or having enough to retire with. If this is essentially what we all desire in the free parts of the world then take that thought to the table when meeting your customers. What do they want? The same as us. They do not want to pay more for something than it's worth.

They do not want to be taken advantage of because they don't understand everything about the product. They want to trust in someone enough that not only will they keep coming back for services but recommend those same services and that same helpful, kind, caring salesperson to their friends. Will you be that person that understands? Will you be the one person that stands out in your company that never brags, the one who quietly does their work building their character to be like The Holy One and that keeps winning contest after contest without trying, the one who everyone looks to for answers but you know there are no quick answers because they wouldn't believe it if you told them. Pray. Pray for your company, pray for your success, pray for your customers when you are alone, and know what some of them are going through. WHEN WE ASK THE LORD, HE ANSWERS, WE PRAISE, HE BLESSES. This is only a secret because non-believers don't want it to be true. They would rather have some potion, magical incantation, astrological sign or special words to give to the client to make them buy. That's not us. We were created for eternity and in eternity we will have each other. Would you want to just sell something to someone that they neither wanted or needed just to make the sale when that same person could also potentially be in eternity with you? "Do for others what you would want them to do for you." Matthew 7: 12. I call this the golden rule because when you are this kind of Sales Master all you touch seems to turn to gold. And to you it's become the norm. Because all the gold is then used to help others find their way into eternity. This is what becomes the Big Deal!

5
CHAPTER

❖

How People Buy

Because people buy emotionally and not logically it is very difficult for the highly computer literate, or as we call them, Nerds, to become Sales Masters. It is not how they were built. They were meant for other logical great things, to discover and go places we haven't the brain quality to go. That being said we definitely have the ability and desire to sell the stuff they make because almost everyone wants those products they create. When someone shows interest in what you offer then it's that moment to dig deeper into those emotions to uncover their want or need. Let's take a couple of products on the spectrum and go through how the initial sales process should look.

Scenario1* Buying emotionally: You are selling RVs for a midsized dealership and a potential customer comes through the door. You see them and watch their body language. You notice they are looking around but for something specific. You slowly get up from your desk and close out what you're doing then nonchalantly walk over in their direction. You have learned to become a great salesperson and are always mastering your craft. You notice they are sharply dressed, look like they probably have the money to buy the dealership, and seem very friendly. Your heart should feel comfortable because you already see them as potential friends that you wouldn't mind having dinner with or talking over at a cookout. With your hands at your side, you confidently approach your new friends and ask them your first discovery question while looking at them with a smile in your eyes. Speaking in smooth slow tones you say, "Hi,

I'm (Your first name). You seem to know what you're looking for. May I help you find it?" They tell you the type of RV they are looking for so you say, "Yes! We do have this." As you walk them to those options you ask in a clear voice, "What have you heard or seen that attract you to this RV?" They tell you that you are looking for a personal reason to become acquainted. You say, "Those are good qualities about this vehicle." "Do you have older children in other parts of the country?" Personal fact-finding is your first mission to have them like and trust you like you already feel you could like and trust them. They tell you that they do and this is one reason why they are looking. You then tell them of either someone close to you that bought for the same reason or a personal experience. You keep your experience short as what really matters are their needs not your talking.

Getting back to them you state, "This has all of those features you are looking for but did you know it can also do _____?" They like what they hear but are now interested in the price. Knowing that "Price is only an issue in the absence of value" (Tom Hopkins) you are now ready to give them that price because you know they like you and trust you, they have the money, and they are answering all your questions and are ready to buy but there is that one last element. Which will they buy? So, you draw up the 3 options of different features that they could potentially want from the cheapest to the most expensive ones and let them decide. IT'S NOT IF THEY WILL BUY FROM YOU BUT WHICH THEY WILL BUY FROM YOU.

As they sit in front of you and you turn the 3 options over on the table in 1 neat and beautifully designed page you point to each one showing them its features of them. Then, sitting back you simply ask, "Which of these options do you like the best?" Now you wait as long as it takes, making no noise, for their answer. They tell which one and then you ask them a question where "No" means "Yes". So, you ask them, "If you could have this dream machine in your driveway in less than (however many days you know it will take plus 3) is there any reason not to authorize the paperwork right now?" They both exclaim, "No". People love to say, No.

Now you have made the initial part of the sale BUT you fight every emotion in you that is making you feel full of joy and squash it until you really have the sale. When do we really have the sale? When the money is in our account with no chargeback and the customer has either warmly referred us to another or given us a 5-star review. Then you can do your happy dance alone. If you have helped someone, get what they want at a good price and helped the company, even though you are getting paid well, you have done a good deed, my friend. Scripture tells us this about the rewards of good deeds: Don't tell anyone what you have done and greater will be your reward in Paradise. Matthew 6:2-4 "2

When you do something well, do not blow a trumpet before you, as the hypocrites[a] do in the synagogues and in the streets to win the praise of others. Definitely, I say to you, they have received their reward. 3 But when you do something well, do not let your left hand know what your right is doing, 4 so that your good job may be secret. And your Father who sees in secret will repay you." Every time I make a sale it shows on the spreadsheet but I tell no one to accept The Lord. I tell Him in the form of a Biiiiiig. "THANK YOU, LORD!" Bragging about the things that you do tells heaven that you didn't need or appreciate what The Lord has done. You will receive all the accolades you deserve on earth but wouldn't it be great to have some unimaginable never-ending gifts in eternity. Save it up! Master salespeople do not need to brag about themselves their good works speak for themselves.

Scenario2* Keeping logically: You have just sold a new roof to a couple who has been looking for the right company for months. They like you; they trust you they put the down payment in. You know they have potential "Buyers Remorse" because of conversations they've had with you and just the fact that it took them so long to say, "Yes." In order now to not let a moment go by that would make them regret their purchase you systematically send them communications while they wait for the project to begin. Remember you really don't have the sale until it is not chargebackable and they have either given you warm referrals or 5-Star reviews. You also like them and want to make sure they are continually reassured and comfortable in hiring you and the company you represent.

Steps you could do to keep their confidence strong:

1. As soon as they have made that deposit send them an email template that states, "We have received your initial payment and want to thank you for your business. Here are a few people you should know" Then list names, numbers, and emails of important people in the company that will also be communicating with them throughout the project.

2. After a week goes by be sure there is follow-up communication on what has taken place. Either by you or the end sourcing team. Let the customer know that their material has been ordered and they will be contacted when it arrives. A great way to do this is through text notifications

3. A very important personal point to make right here: No matter how you feel; AT THE MOMENT A CUSTOMER CALLS ANSWER THE PHONE QUICKLY AND WHEN YOU KNOW WHO IT IS, SMILE AND BE AS GLAD TO SPEAK WITH THEM AS YOU ARE WITH YOUR BEST FRIEND YOU HAVEN'T HEARD FROM IN YEARS. This goes for no matter what type of customer they are or how difficult they may be. Always be glad to hear from them.

4. Sometimes it takes longer for the product to arrive or there may be backups due to a storm season where there are a lot of customers to get to. A week later send another message letting the customer know of any issues due to unforeseen circumstances and reassure them they are still in line moving up. If your company has a system to tell the customer what place in line, they are in, then they can see one week to the next what their spot is and they are moving up. Visuals are a great tool.

5. Continue to follow up each week even if the only thing you can tell them is their new place in line.

6. If ever there are issues like weather delays or other things that have been out of the company's control just text or call and let the customer know what is going on.

    People are anxious about the purchase they have made and in this age of technology want to know you have not forgotten about them when a simple communication can handle it. If a company is not keeping the customer in the loop it shouts out loud, "We don't care about you we only want your money." This is taken as highly unprofessional and will destroy a company's reputation if it continues.

7. The product is in and ready for delivery or the crew is ready for the job. The customer then receives an Email AND a Text message from you to let them know when the job will start and approximately how long it will take (or when the product will be delivered and how long it will take to assemble). Keeping in the adage of under-promising and

over-delivering you add a day to the length of time you believe it will take to complete the job or an hour in the case of a machine.

8. Job is complete and the customer is so happy because if there were any issues you handled them immediately. Now, you ask for the final payment by saying, "How would you like to pay the balance?" and mention the various ways and forms to make payment.

9. They are still not a customer! Yet. Why? By now you understand. They must either give you warm referrals or leave a positive 5-Star review online. So, you ask. This is best done by Text message nowadays but few will prefer other means of communication. "It was a real pleasure working with you through this whole process. A big once-in-a-lifetime purchase like this can sometimes be very stressful. I am glad you are happy with the outcome like we are. Would you please show how satisfied you are with the job we have done by sharing a couple of names and numbers of others that may have a hard time finding a trustworthy company like ours?" "If it's not too much to ask would you also mind bragging about us with a 5-Star review simply by clicking this link?" "Again, it was really nice to work for you and we hope to work for you on another project you may need soon."

6

CHAPTER

❖

Realistic Expectations

Not every job goes wonderfully smooth. Not every customer will love the work or the processes they have to go through. There will be complaints if you are successful at all. With these customers, we live and learn. The right way to always work is with genuine integrity. Always care about the customer even when they have created a voodoo doll at your home of you and are pricking it with needles. Pray for them because you may be the only agent of the divine, they will run into. Stand in the gap for them if you see they are in great spiritual need. Usually, I find this with few people who either have anger, anxiety, or depression issues. This means don't' take their issues personally unless there are company problems that need to be resolved.

You may have been sent by The Lord just to reach out to them in their time of need other than buying your product. Care about them even if it seems they hate the world.

As Master Salespeople we will paint a picture in the minds of our customers that will be realistic and obtainable. If you want to shoot yourself in the foot just say things like, "This is the best deal since the resurrection of Jesus." When we speak unrealistically it shows us grasping at straws in order to make a sale. This is the mistake the first-year salespeople do. The Master at sales will know, in their mind, that problems could happen and are wondering in advance of some issues that could happen with this customer. Then with that truth in mind will say something like, "The reason I work here is that (one great reason you work for this company and not their competitor)." "Not everything is perfect all the time but you can be sure our hearts are in the right place." John Addison CEO Primerica. And, although we are not perfect, we are striving to get there. I trust you will enjoy working with us as we hope to with you. What do you say?"

Setting realistic expectations by being honest and down-to-earth will keep you real. People like doing business with real honest companies. Wouldn't you agree? Let them know that any unavoidable issues that come up will be handled in the most professional way. "That's what I'm here for." You reassure the customer. As a Sales Professional, your job isn't done when you just make the sale.

What makes your company different than your competitors should be foremost in your speech. There may be 2 or there may be 200 other companies the customer could go to and purchase what you have to sell. The reason they will become a lifelong customer of this company is that you have clearly given them a reason to. What makes your service/product different that they would want to buy it and buy you? Really. Do you know? Write it down here, then in one year, write it down again and see how it changes.

Today's date: _____

Why should I buy this product/service from this company?

_____

_____.

Why should I buy it from you?

_____

_____

One year's later or more date: _____

Why should I buy this product/service from this company?

_____

_____.

Why should I buy it from you?

_____

_____

Being realistic gives you the ability to under-promise and over-deliver. Being realistic does not give you the right to trash yourself or your company. They do not need to know all the flaws in your life or the improvements that your company still has to make unless they point it out. If that happens then freely agree with them and let them know you are working on that to become better and better. There is balance and imperfections in all of us. If you are having a bad day there is hope. The sun will rise anew tomorrow. We will talk about balance and peace in a little bit. But before we do we need to talk about one more thing that all salespeople and business owners must come to terms with. I guarantee that once you come to terms with this attitude towards what you do it will be like turning a corner into a better future of peace and calmness. Here it is.

Accept the Law of Large Numbers:

This is one of the most difficult things for us to swallow because we all think that "if only we had this or if only I did that then everyone would buy." That will never happen. Come to terms with the truth right now and you can design your business and sales approach with a happier state of mind. The good news is that you can determine your sales average and better scale your business. You can predict how much could be sold, how much you could make, and how much the company can grow. The Law of Large numbers works across the board in almost every aspect of sales and service.

I'm going to give you the numbers and once you see them look back over the last year and see if this natural rule isn't true for you.

100/10/4/1

Out of 100 people you contact face to face 10 will show an interest, 4 will say they are going to buy and 1 will actually become a satisfied customer. Those are the large numbers. Let's take a look at the small averages. It took 4 people to say they would buy for 1 of them to buy. It took 10 people to show an interest for 4 to say they were very interested. It took 100 face-to-face contacts for 10 to even show an interest.

Now, check your personal sales numbers. Remember, this is the law of LARGE numbers. If you are only looking back to less than 10 contacts the numbers will be off a smidge. Once we accept these numbers we know how to thrive, how to work, and never diminish ourselves or the product again. "Don't Worry, Be Happy" will become true when you say, "Yes!" to the numbers.

Now, let me show you where there will be skewed. This will help if you are a sales manager or business owner to know where the salespeople are that need the most encouragement. The worst of the worst people, I mean those that should not even be in sales will make at least 1 sale out of every 10 potentials that say they are very interested. The average and ordinary salesperson will sell 2 out of every 10 very interested potentials. The really good salesperson will sell 3 out of every 10 very interested potentials. The Sales Master, the top 1 percenter will sell a wonderful 4 out of every 10 potential customers that are very interested. I know, I know. Some of you are thinking as I thought my first few years as a business owner and sales manager that those numbers are not good enough. I know it hurts a little and stings the pride a bunch but, this is why you must come to terms with them. For as long as you are not happy with those numbers is the length of days you will be an emotionally miserable person. Accept the numbers and be happy. Work with those average and good salespeople to get them to become great. Take your great ones and make them managers if you haven't already.

The 2 suitcases

There are 2 metaphorical suitcases that a salesperson takes with them everywhere they go.

The 1st suitcase is the salesperson become better at their craft of selling. Becoming better at understanding people and their characteristics., better at holding their tongue and waiting for the right moments to speak, better at having people like and trust you in 90 seconds or less, and better at asking questions to get to the pain points of the potential customer, and better at being comfortable in their own skin as someone who helps people get what they desire. They are essentially becoming a master at their craft. The art of real salesmanship.

The 2nd suitcase that every salesperson takes with them is understanding and becoming knowledgeable of the item that is being purchased by them. Knowing your item for sale is important but of more importance is the 1st suitcase. If you are no good with people it matters not how much you know. Remember, "People do not care how much you know until they know how much you care." Art Williams AL Willams

If you are fresh in a new company and beginning to learn the product but are already good with sales you may have learned already a technique that helps you with a customer when they ask you a question you do not know the answer to. Never make stuff up to try to sound like you know what you're talking about. People may not know you are talking from what you don't know but they will feel there is something wrong and because of that emotional discomfort will not make the purchase from you.

This is the reason for Sales Managers. They should know about the products being sold and are supposed to help you close the deal. Therefore, use them to help you. This is how to best utilize a sales manager: A customer asks you about the product and you come to the extent of your knowledge and cannot answer the question. You have already created a good relationship with them where they like and trust you and you feel confident, they will make the purchase from you so you say, "Mr. & Mrs. Gonzalez I know a lot about this product but you stumped me with this question. Would you like for me to get that answer for you right now or within the next 24d hours?

By knowing that you can ask this question it releases the stress from having to know everything about the product and keeps your sales process smoother. If the customer says, "We would really like to know that before we move any further, "then pick up the phone, call your sales manager/trainer, tell them you have a kind couple in front of you and they have a quick question, then hand your phone over to the one who asked the question. If, however, they said that the answer would be fine within 24 hours then once you are finished with the sales discussion, get the answer and then get it to them within 12 hours.

After all is said and done be sure to know how to answer that question for the next time it is asked. Remember, "When someone ask you a question answer it then ask them a question right back." This keeps you in charge of the conversation.

Know thy Maker

Most likely, if you are reading this book, you believe in something. A higher form of power, a divine being, a creator of the universe, or an all-knowing Spirit(s). The reason I believe in The One True and living God of the scriptures is that all of His inspired prophecies of the future so far have been 100% accurate. Looking at the books of Isaiah, Ezekiel, and Daniel. Those things that The Lord said would happen happened right when they were supposed to happen. Then when the promised one came, He came to earth right on prophetic time. We have Revelations that tell us some things that have happened in recent history and things that are about to happen before the end of this age. Because this is primarily a guidebook about the Faith in Sales I will keep the Bible study with dates and specifics out of this book.

The purpose for me explaining the facts of scripture is because that is the basis of our belief in the eternal One. The Omniscient (all Knowing), The Omnipotent (all Powerful), the

Omnipresent (Present everywhere), Omnibenevolent (all Perfect or all Loving). Wow! What a God to serve.

It was always difficult for me growing up to just do what I was told. I needed reasons. Succumbing to authority was difficult because it was just doing what the law states just because it's the law. Needing to know why before I obeyed then became an issue for me. Though it has been a slow and difficult road I worship this God without question or reservations because of what I have learned and mostly what I have experienced. Every day, literally, comes another way that He shows His mercy and kindness towards me. Because of Him I am successful. Because of Him I am Happy, Because of Him my life is complete, I know who I am, peace has come to me, joy is abundant, and there is a life after this that will be worth living in for eternity.

To know The Lord requires a process of personal growth and learning. That's it! Sounds too simple, doesn't it? Getting to know Him is like staying friends with someone or staying in a loving married relationship. These cannot be taken for granted. There is a concerted effort that must take place on everyone's part. One of the coolest things about that work of knowing thy maker is that The Lord is always doing His part. It's us who slack on putting in the time and energy with the relationship. "Why don't we just naturally have a terrific relationship already built-in us"? You might think. I mean If He is Omniscient and Omnipotent why isn't that just part of our biological nature to have a solid relationship of everlasting love with our Creator? Great question. The reason is because we were created in His image, and He has given us (not the animals, fish, or other living things) the ability to decide with our own conscience whether to love Him or not. Lucifer's biggest complaint in Heaven was that God was not fair, that His laws were not for everyone, and that we should be able to do whatever we want to make ourselves feel good. God has put this world on the stage of the Universe for all thinking beings to be able to determine for themselves if He is in the right or if the Devil is right.

How do we know The Lord in the close way that He wants us to? First, ask Him. Matthew 7:7 Every one of us was created with a unique design. We do have many features and tendencies of our parents but not one person that has ever been created or ever will be created is just like YOU. The Lord made you different and special in your own way in His image because He is so creative and unboring. He loves diversity, design, creativity, and exploration. "We are fearfully and wonderfully made." Psalm 139:14. His love for you is so strong that He is willing to pay whatever the price is to have you be with Him throughout the ceaseless ages. John 3:16.

There is no other love that is like God's love. Your soul will never be satisfied with all the money in the world or all the friends in the world. Being the most famous person will not bring peace to your soul that only He can bring. John 14:27. Once you really know Him you can then truly trust Him because The Lord will never let you down. Hebrews 13:5. He cares more about your happiness, and your emotional state of mind than you even know to care about. He desires for you to be successful in life. Proverbs 3:1-4, 1 Kings 2:3. Do you want peace in your life? Do you desire to be filled with a lasting joy that the world cannot understand? Keep reading

8
CHAPTER

❖

A Day in the Life of Faith & Sales

It has taken me a long painful journey to learn the things that I know. The whole reason I wrote this book is so that sales and faith will not be so taxing on you as it was for me. Loving parents correct and guide their children from wrong to right in order to help make life better for their children than it was for them. Good friends will also tell you directly when you are headed on the wrong path because they want what is best for you. I don't want anyone to have to struggle uphill like I had to unless it is absolutely necessary for them to get it through their thick skull as I did.

Here is the day in my life that I had to learn through the school of "Hard Knox" to get to where I am and keep moving.

First thing in the morning when waking up is to thank the Lord for a comfortable place to sleep.

Next, while showering, eating breakfast, and getting ready for the day have soft delightful music in the background to put my mind in the right space

Next, read selected passages of scripture and specifically ready the Proverbs for the day. (Proverbs has 30 chapters one for each day)

Next, going to my secret place where only myself and God are to talk: Tell Him my fears, joys, worries, and church, and family concerns. Then with Him about business issues and personal issues so that both of them will improve. I pray for anyone that He puts in the front of my mind. Lastly, I ask Him that "all that I touch today may turn to gold that I may glorify You in front of others."

We then have family worship where we all meet daily at the same time in the morning briefly before everyone heads off to their daily lives. Prayer, hugs, kiss the spouse, and goodbyes.

While driving to work I allow my mind to reminisce over all that happened that morning. I tell God out loud how thankful I am to have all that He has provided. I remember when I didn't even know Him and how bleak and unimportant life was for me. "God, you are so good to me. Thank you for my wonderful life."

At work, I turn on the pleasant music (because hard music interferes with the brain receptors and makes it difficult to concentrate).

Quickly I write down the 6-10 reasonable things that will be accomplished today

As those items are accomplished, I thank The Lord and check them off

Before any appointment, I send up a quick prayer that "all will go smooth and that your words be in my mouth so that I may not offend but be a minister of hope to them." "Please help me to uncover all the needs they may have and design the best proposal for them so that they may be satisfied, the company is benefitted, and I will be successful." He reminds me to ask that all I touch may turn to gold and a smile crosses over my face.

Just before I meet with the customers, I tell myself to "cool it". I get nervous easily of the unknown no matter how many times I've done it. Every person is different therefore it is always kind of new. (Great reason to fall in love with sales).

After meeting with them I create an amazing proposal that will meet their needs. How? I breathe in God and breathe out self. Being a little dyslexic, I have to know everything like the back of my hand or it's like I've never seen it before. After the proposal is done it is really only a rough draft.

Briefly closing my eyes, I ask The Lord to please tell me what is wrong that must be fixed. Slowly going over it I keep my mind stayed on Him. Isaiah 26:3. He softly nudges me to look at this or that and tells me how to perfect it.

Once it is completed, I ask Him one more time if anything needs to be corrected. I wait and if there is a warm signal in my heart of hearts, I tell Him, "Thank you. I could not have done it without you."

Now I go over the details with the customer and ask them leading questions so that they may pick the best option for them.

The sale has begun when they pay the down payment. I then praise Him quietly. Should anyone ask how things are going I tell them God is so good.

On the way home I praise Him for the day. I tell my spouse how God has led me throughout the day. And listen as she tells me about her day.

We have dinner and just before bed all the TVs, games, phones, and other devices are turned off as we meet together once again. We know each has our own special spiritual book to read outside of the Bible and read quietly to ourselves for 30 minutes. (Before the kids were teenagers, we would read Storytime books to them).

We then get ready for bed and spend our personal time with God before going to sleep.

Somewhere in the middle of the night, I seem to lose my emotional high with God and in the morning must get up and spend that personal time with Him again.

I know someone reading this right now is saying, "That's a fantasy land". "I can't do that". You don't have to have a spouse or children to do all of these things with you and God. You can do this but you must take that first step. If you have never done any of these things before and don't even know if you believe why not make the first step by simply saying, "Lord, I don't believe, help my unbelief". Did you know that "Prayer is the opening of the heart to God as to a friend?" E.G. White. Become friends with God by first just talking to Him. He will guide you into all truth. John 16:13

There is a successful formula that I have found between me and The Lord that works for us. It may work for you. It's P.A.P.B. I Pray, He Answers, I Praise, He Blesses. The blessings are always happening because He continually takes care of me but there are added blessings that come from Him. I believe He gives them in a special way to encourage us to keep moving in the right direction with our abiding relationship with Him. Let me put this formula into a practical scenario.

9

CHAPTER

❖

Sing Praises to Him

You are a residential door-to-door salesperson. Before you even start knocking of doors or even pick a neighborhood you pray. You ask The Lord to lead you to the right neighborhood and to the right doors where you can help meet the needs of someone looking for what you have. You wait just a moment for Him to gently guide you to the right area. While continuing to listen to that "still small voice" you remember that He told you He would take care of you today and make everything you touch turn to gold. You have a sense that a certain neighborhood needs your product in their homes more than any other and it's just around the corner. You make sure everything about you is presentable and begin knocking on doors and leaving your brochures/cards. Soon the first door opens to your knocks and asks how they may help you. You tell them you were  sent there because you felt impressed that they were in need of what you have "But before we look at options; have you been in the area long?" "Where were you before here?" "Oh, I'm from _____ and am now living just over there." "Would you like to talk about this option or this option?" With your comfortable heart, knowing The Lord is taking care of everything you ask if it "would be better for us to talk inside?" There you go over options and continue making them like and trust you as you are getting to know and like them. In the whole sales conversation, you find out that they have a physical or spiritual need and that you have been given the opportunity to help them by praying for and with them right there.

Warning: Never use kindness or spirituality as a means to pretend you are sympathizing with someone you do not even care about. If you truly do not care about them either pass the sale over to someone that will work better with them or just work on getting them what they need.

But here you did make a friendly connection and feel confident that they are not only moving forward with the installation but will give you referrals to more customers. Now what? Now you praise. Praise the Lord for what He has done. What did He just do? 1. He listened to your need and answered by sending you to the right place at the right time. 2. He gave you a signed contract. Yes, you put yourself out there and followed His promptings but He led you all the way. 3. You may have made a new friend. 4. He made you part of His Ministry of Mercy and was an instrument to lift someone in need.

Now, that you praise Him between you and Him the next time someone asks, "How's it goin'?" You can tell them how The Lord has given you a role to help people and how He answered your prayers. Soon warm referrals begin to call you directly because they are in need of your product or service and only want to work with you because of the kindness you showed to their friend or family. And, He keeps on blessing you.

If you have a child or take care of a child then you understand. A child that is always excited and wants to share with you how things are going in their life makes you just want to scoop them up and give all your love and attention to them, including gifts. You think about that child when you are shopping for yourself and see something you know they would just love or something they need and get it for them. You give them the gift and if that child says, "Thank you, thank you, thank you so much. I love it!" Do you know what you want to do? You want to spoil them crazy. In fact, as a good person, you do all you can to withhold from spoiling them. That's how The Lord feels about you when you Pray and when you Praise. He desires more and more for you and sometimes can't help Himself from spoiling you. Remember, He is emotional.

Here are the ancient texts to back this formula up:

We Pray, He Answers:

John 14:14 " If you [a]ask anything in My name, I will do *it."*

Luke 11:9-13"So I say to you, ask, and it will be given to you; seek, and you will find; knock, and it will be opened to you. For everyone who asks, receives; and he who seeks, finds; and to him who knocks, it will be opened. Now suppose one of you fathers is asked by his son for a fish; he will not give him a snake instead of a fish, will he?

John 15:7 "If you abide in Me, and My words abide in you, ask whatever you wish, and it will be done for you."

1 John 3:22 "and whatever we ask we receive from Him, because we keep His commandments and do the things that are pleasing in His sight."

1 John 5:14 "This is the confidence which we have before Him, that, if we ask anything according to His will, He hears us."

We Praise, He Blesses: Psalm 28:7 "The Lord *is* my strength and my shield;
My heart trusted in Him, and I am helped;
Therefore my heart greatly rejoices,
And with my song, I will praise Him."

Ephesians 1:3 "Blessed *be* the God and Father of our Lord Jesus Christ, who has blessed us with every spiritual blessing in the heavenly *places* in Christ,"

Proverbs 3:5-6 "Trust in the LORD with all your heart,
And lean not on your own understanding;
In all your ways acknowledge Him,
And He shall [a]direct your paths."

Psalm 37:4 "Delight yourself also in the LORD,
And He shall give you the desires of your heart."

Heaven is moved by the praises from the lips of one of God's children.
The demons shudder at the sound of singing to The Lord and The Holy Ones of Heaven join in the singing. After the praises comes a shower of blessing. Gloom is lifted and a bounty of hope is restored. Ruth 2:12 "May the LORD reward your work, and may your wages be full from the LORD, the God of Israel, under whose wings you have come to take refuge."

With the attitude of these praises comes a spirit of contentment in perfecting the work so that the praise given next time will be that much stronger. Master your craft at every opportunity. This desire should become natural as the Masters of Sales are drawn to honing their abilities. Abilities to become better and quicker and more professional when helping others get what they need.

10
CHAPTER

Prove your gratefulness

In proving your gratitude to God, you are making a few strong statements. None of them is, "I'm doing this because The Lord told me I had to". By proving you are grateful for what He has done you are telling yourself that He is the giver of all good things, that He will continue to provide even when things look bleak. You are also telling the world that The Lord is worthy of what little He has required and however much, you are willing to give back.

This is a difficult issue with new believers and a settled issue with the seasoned. God asks us to give Him 10% of our "first fruits". This means we give Him 10% of all the Gross income we receive. How you give it is directly for the upbuilding and strengthening of His Church and Its Ministry. This is the tithe that is required without question. But the offerings are given out of your resources from the abundance of your heart. I have always given the tithe but I have learned over the years something interesting. I have learned that I could not Out Give The Lord. I mean, if I happened to give him too much and it wasn't prudent for that week/month then He turns around and gives it right back to me. Every couple of years my wife and I decide to increase the percentage of our giving and interestingly enough our income increase right along with it.

Don't let this be a hard pill to swallow. Try the Lord and see if He will not open the windows of Heaven and bless you more than you ever thought possible. Malachi 3:10 This process of giving back to The Lord is the strongest thing that keeps a good person not just right but humble. In this world where everyone wants to give and get a "That-a-boy" the best way to stand up straight with confidence is to receive it from our Creator. We are good because He makes us good. Without Him, all our best efforts are like the filthiest of rags. Prove to the universe that you are settled in this matter. Show them all that you trust completely in Him and become a person that is wonderful in the eyes of both Heaven and Earth.

When we work for God (The Lord) we quit being a "Yes-Man" to people, especially those that write out our paychecks. "For the LORD detests the perverse but takes the upright into his confidence." Proverbs 3:32. When we are commissioned or 1099 (in the USA) that means we work essentially for ourselves because we don't get paid until we bring in that sale. Because of this, we must trust The Lord and not ourselves. No more of this, telling the owners or managers of the company you are selling for, what they want to hear. You know "What are you going to sell this week/month? What are your goals? Where do you see yourself at the end of the year?" All of these questions are good for the company because it helps push others that are not with The Lord and need that earthly thought process. Yet with Him, we are a majority. We might not be able to give the number of how much because He hasn't given it yet, but you can tell them, "I put my head down and work with all my might and God will make up any difference."

God is not a loser. When you put your business in His hands, He will work everything out right. You must do all you can with all your best effort and then watch as everything not only happens on time but continues year after year to get better and better. Only trust and obey His promptings. What you are going to see happen in your sales will not only astound you but possibly bring envy to the other salespeople. If they are not envious and they have a pure heart they will begin asking you how. "How do you do it month after month breaking all the sales berries?" When this happens are you going to give them an expose on how wonderful you are? No! This is the moment when God Shines. Tell them how God has led you. Tell them what He has done for you. Testify! Glorify Him now openly and without hesitation. "I cannot count the times when you have faithfully rescued me... I will tell everyone how good you are and of your constant, daily care. [16] I walk in the strength of the Lord God. I tell everyone that you alone are just and good." Psalms 71:15-16. Remember we do not brag about our works on earth because we are waiting for something special in the hereafter. Keep our heads in heaven while our feet are on the ground. In this way, The Lord will promote you. "The wise are promoted to honor, but fools are promoted to shame!" Proverbs 3:35

11
CHAPTER

❖

Beautiful Balance

The challenges of life are sometimes surmounting; Finances, Health, Family, Relationships, Work, and Church. Then there are emotional struggles; Career pressures, Unfair treatment, Emptiness, Boredom, Confusion, Anxiety, bouts of depression, and sometimes apathy. Being able to have balance with everything could feel like you are a clown on a unicycle spinning chainsaws while bouncing a grenade on your nose. Or you could have everything under control and when things happen that are out of your control you know exactly what to do.

You have probably heard it before how many wealthy people spend their whole life acquiring their worth but at the end of life, they spend it all on their health. No one wants to be that person. Life could feel like a game of Russian Roulette or the tide of life could feel like normal ups and downs with occasional big opportunities and mishaps. I say we "hedge the bet" and be prepared for things to come. My grandpa used to tell me, "Expect the best but prepare for the worst." This told me growing up that I could be joyful for the future but at the same time plan for potential problems. Let's be filled with hope and plan to be better with every passing day.

Your health is your wealth. Regarding emotional health; I have found that anxiety or depression settles into my bones when I spend too much time thinking about issues that could be handled without too much thought. There are a couple of sayings to help drive home the point. "Don't make a mountain of a molehill." "Whatever you meditate on all day long that becomes your reality." "Worry means you suffer twice." Doesn't it make sense? Whatever you give most attention to is what rules your life because it takes up most of the space in your mind. I said "in" your mind because our thoughts are actually powerful. What we think continuously about actually makes creased patterns of neurons in our brains. The path of these neurons then becomes easier and easier to take the more that we take them. It's like walking on a grassy pathway over and over every day until it is a well-worn road. (see https://www.khanacademy.org/science/biology/human-biology/neuron-nervous-system/a/neurotransmitters-their-receptors) Here it talks about Neurotransmitters, Synaptic Vesicles, Receptors, and Postsynaptic Neurons). That's why we should not go down the road of continuous negative thought patterns. Psychologically if we do not want to feel those unhappy emotions and end up a basket case when we should be seeing success in every part of our lives, then we must learn to turn our thoughts in the right direction. Do not let your own mind sabotage your success.

How do we change the malicious thought patterns that sometimes ruin our lives? Even Aristotle had the answer well before any neuroscience discovered it. He wrote, "We are what we repeatedly do; excellence, then, is not an act but a habit." We must make it a daily habit to improve ourselves with the power of God. It has been easy to destroy ourselves but now we must begin the real construction of our minds and actions. It's time to fix our wayward characters.

"WE CANNOT SOLVE OUR PROBLEMS WITH THE SAME THINKING WE USED WHEN WE CREATED THEM." Albert Einstein. We were created in His Image so that we have the amazing ability to choose. Animals, plants, and every other thing on earth that can make a decision make it based on pain or reward. We, God's children, were created on a higher plane. We decide if we will accept certain things into our lives. We choose what we are going to believe, and we develop our response and reaction systems. We may have been born with certain genes or brought up to react certain ways in specific situations but, Thanks be to God, we do not have to stay that way. This is good news for the salesperson. It means that if you are built by God to be a "people person" you can become a Sales Master. It's all a choice of the mind that leads to proper actions. We choose to do what we must regardless of the negative thoughts that whisp through our minds and slothful feelings that come over us. We get up and go anyways. Like Daniel, we "purpose in our hearts" to do what is right.

How do you change what you are? If you haven't figured it out yet, The Lord has the answers. The Lord desires greater things for you than you can imagine. "For **my** thoughts are **not your** thoughts, neither are **your ways my ways**," says the LORD. "As the heavens are **higher than** the earth, so are **my ways higher than your ways** and **my** thoughts than **your** thoughts." Isaiah 55:8-9. If He wants more for you than you can imagine why not give your entire sales process over to Him. Let Him Rule!

Because of the neurotransmitters that science has recently discovered in our brains, it is understood how we can make character changes in our lives. In his book "Think and Grow Rich" Napoleon Hill explains "Thought Impulses". Here he accurately states, "Man can create nothing which he does not first conceive in the form of an impulse of thought." Page 200. He says this after explaining that people will live in fear of old age and fear of death and let it run their lives." God, of course, knew this because He created our brains and understands how sin and degradation have settled into them. He wants us to have a higher train of thought and reasoning that will elevate us above our moral decline. Our thoughts lead our brain and from our brain, we speak our thoughts then we put those things we are talking about into action. Continuous actions build habits and our habits create our life of who we are. This all starts with thought impulses. What thought impulses will we hover over? What thoughts will we nourish and let thrive so that ultimately these become our life and belief system?

Do you want to become an excellent person? Not just a kind person but an excellent person that is thought highly of by both God and People? The Lord has the answer to your brain dilemma.

'And now, dear brothers and sisters, one final thing. Fix your thoughts on what is true, honorable, right, pure, lovely, and admirable. Think about things that are excellent and worthy of praise." Philippians 4:8. For the same reason that your mother told you to stay away from certain people when you were a teen is the same reason we need to stick with Jesus. Talk with Him, read about Him, tell others about Him, and praise Him because "By beholding we become changed." 2 Cor. 3:18.

You know what is most important in someone's life because their tendencies are to talk about it, spend money on it, and go to it for every up and down emotion they feel. When we worship The Holy One of heaven, He is the one we go to. He says, "Come and let us reason together…" Isaiah 1:18 and it is our privilege to talk and reason with The Lord at any time. He has a 24/7/365 open door policy. How amazing is that? He cares about our success in life, relationships, money, family, business, health, and all other things than we do. No matter how small the need He wants to help. No matter how insurmountable the obstacle He has the power to overcome it for and with you. Give your best to Him and He will make up for the lacking difference.

Emotional Health

The Cure for Anxiety Matthew 6: 25"For this reason, I say to you, do not be worried about your life, *as to* what you will eat or what you will drink; nor for your body, *as to* what you will put on. Is not life more than food, and the body more than clothing? **26**"Look at the birds of the air, that they do not sow, nor reap nor gather into barns, and *yet* your heavenly Father feeds them. Are you not worth much more than they? **27**"And who of you by being worried can add a *single* hour to his life? **28**"And why are you worried about clothing? Observe how the lilies of the field grow; they do not toil nor do they spin, **29**yet I say to you that not even Solomon in all his glory clothed himself like one of these. **30**"But if God so clothes the grass

of the field, which is *alive* today and tomorrow is thrown into the furnace, *will He* not much more *clothe* you? You of little faith! **31**"Do not worry then, saying, 'What will we eat?' or 'What will we drink?' or 'What will we wear for clothing?' **32**"For the Gentiles eagerly seek all these things; for your heavenly Father knows that you need all these things. **33**"But seek first His kingdom and His righteousness, and all these things will be added to you. **34**"So do not worry about tomorrow; for tomorrow will care for itself. Each day has enough trouble of its own."

Body Health

If you are having trouble getting to sleep, I will give you the answer. If your body is overweight, there's a wonderful solution. If you are emotionally exhausted, you don't have to be anymore. To become a Sales Master these things in your life must be under control. Here are the answers.

Sleep: When I was a child I would stay up late at night until early in the morning just staring at the dark ceiling and wondering if I would ever get to sleep. 10 PM would come and I knew it every night because the old train would come through town and blow its eerie whistle one long then two short steamy blows. The fact is I knew everything going on when I should have been fast asleep. Finally, I decided it was time to figure this out or my whole life would be troubling every night. I began talking to God.

God showed me that the reason I couldn't sleep is that my head was too full of thoughts. I would think about how late it was and then be scared that I would be too sleepy the next day to do well in school. I'd worry about my grades. I'd think about the future. I wondered about the girl I liked and if she liked me or my friend instead. I'd just lay there and think about whatever came to mind and let it wistfully control my thoughts. Then it hit me. It made was making complete sense. I had to stop the madness!

I figured out that I needed to take control of my thoughts so that I could get to sleep. This is how I did it. To teach you the basics now and get you on the right path to restful nights. As you lay there first make sure you are rightfully comfortable. Your pillow should be under your head in a way that it is slightly over your shoulders. Tuck yourself in by rolling up one side and then the other so the covers swaddle your body. Now take all the ideas swirling around in your head and tell them that they are all very important and that you will deal with each one at the right time but for tonight you are only going to spend your thoughts on this one issue. Every other thought goes to the back burner to be dealt with at another time. Then ask God to help you as you think about this one thing.

As you lie there working out the one and only issue, you will find yourself quickly falling asleep but we first need to back up. Let's go back to before you even got into bed. You must have settling down routine. Do not eat anything at least 3 hours before laying down. Whole books are written about why. Keep your mind on calm things by listening to soft music without a syncopated rhythm. Have a book that you are reading ½ hour before laying down. Do not watch TV or be scrolling any device as the light flickering will keep your circadian rhythm in a mood that it's time to get up and do something. Now that you have developed a great habit of going to bed it's time to get in. If you make your bed every morning it is so much nicer to get between those sheets at night.

If tension from the day just won't let your heart settle down here is a way to take charge and make it calm once again. While you are laying down in the correct comfortable position, starting from the very top of your head and moving slowly down your body you will tense and hold for 5 seconds then relax. Tense your ears, hold, then relax. Tense up your lips, hold, relax. Tense your chin and relax. Your neck, your shoulders, your arms, fingers, chest. Work your way all the way to your toes. You may only have to do this a few times until you have full control of when and how quickly you go to sleep.

You will take charge of your sleep and this will give you freedom and energy you never thought you could have again. This will give new life to your body and to your brain. Your thought patterns will be clearer as you not only speak with The Lord but as you are on the sales floor and writing up estimates and proposals. Everything in your life will seem to be being managed so much more smoothly.

Eat: If you have been a Christian for a while, you have definitely heard the verse "Your body is the temple of the Holy Spirit." But we rationalize it away when it comes to what we put into it. Many believe that only talk about the exterior and keep it from physical harm or that we should just simply exercise more. We even misquote scripture when it comes to food by using the story of Peter and the sheet and the angle saying, "Kill and eat for all I have made is good" without reading the full text. That was not about food at all it was about taking the message to the rest of the world other than the Jews. So, getting down to brace tacks is this. Stop eating what we know hurts our bodies and brains and start eating what we know is good for them.

Why did Jesus go into the wilderness for 40 days to prepare for His ministry? Because He knows that appetite is the biggest emotional temptation there is. After being famished for 40 days He was still able to reject the temptation of turning the rock into bread. The Devil doesn't even have to tempt most of us. We just eat it because it tastes good. This is the hands-down, absolute wrong way of living. In fact, Alister Crowley's Satanic message's first rule is to "Do as you please for this is the whole of the law." Completely opposite of what God shows us. We must learn to do the will of The Lord even when it goes against our own selfish desires. Start today to cut out some things that are bad and put in things that are good. Believe me, your taste bud will change! God created all the fruit of the earth for us to enjoy.

Move: If you are out of breath after walking up a couple of flights of stairs you know you are out of shape. Your heart is weak and needs to become strong again. The answer isn't "Just go exercise more." Forget that thought. And the answer isn't "Just go on a diet". No, those only work for a minute. The answer is "I must change my life." Begin to see every physical obstacle as an opportunity. What does that mean? When you are going to find a parking space and have to get out of the vehicle and walk all around the store make this obstacle an opportunity and park towards the back of the parking lot and briskly walk to the door. Each time you do this see if you can make it faster, without running, and every time be less out of breath. Here are some other obstacles that are really opportunities:

Stairs: Hit each stair in the same constant motion all the way to the top

Hill: Walk constantly up the hill never running, unless you are out on a run.

Picking up: Set your feet a little further apart, keep your back straight, and squat straight down

Cooking: Instead of piling all your ingredients in your arms and dumping them on the table only take one ingredient at a time at a constant pace

Cleaning: Set staging points that you will not take a break until this section is spic and span. Then as you get healthier make that section of the task larger.

Sitting: Never plop down on a chair, sofa, or bed. Control your muscle movements with consistency in movement. You are in charge of your muscles gaining strength and of your passions to not take way over your self-control.

Watching: Watch less of entertaining screens and get out, move your body and watch more of God's ever-changing creation around you. There are many things that He has created just for your pleasure to see and hear.

12
CHAPTER

Brain Health

Being the control center that has the potential to make everything good or bad in our life we must protect our minds. "Above all else, guard your heart, for everything you do flows from it." Proverbs 4:23. Did you know that some people die of illnesses that are obtained simply because they thought they had them? Our minds are so powerful. They can make or break us. Having a positive mental attitude isn't just a thing to have when you are selling but in every part of your life. Health starts in the mind and then continue in your actions. Why not be an instrument in the hands of God that brings good news and peace to those who are suffering rather than being part of those who are suffering?

"Disease is sometimes produced, and is often greatly aggravated, by the imagination. Many are lifelong invalids who might be well if they only thought so. Many imagine that very slight exposure will cause illness, and its evil effect is produced because it is expected. Many die from disease the cause of which is wholly imaginary." "Courage, hope, faith, sympathy, and love, promote health and prolong life. A contented mind, a cheerful spirit, is health to the body and strength to the soul…" EGW Ministry of Healing p. 241

We must protect our minds by what we watch, hear, and see. Do you remember being a kid and your parents would cover your eyes or ears when something bad was about to happen?

Why not do that for ourselves when we know we are about to see or hear something that will affect our brains. Leave the area so your mind does not have to learn to be tolerant of evil.

Down Time

As salespeople, we all know there are those moments throughout the year when we must give it all we've got. The push to close it all out or clear the "Pipe-Line" is a demand from our companies and from ourselves so that we can see the continued personal growth and company security. But there are those normal times during the week that we must siesta.

Family Time

If you don't take this time every week with your family regret and remorse will quickly pile up and could cause later depression in your life when you wake up out of your drive to financially succeed. We cannot give ourselves to the all-mighty job and tell our families, "But, everything I do I do it for you". They are not buying it anymore. Our families need us too. They need us to be there for them when life happens. There are things in life that are not worth missing simply because you could possibly, maybe get another sale. If this is too difficult to grasp then it's time to plan. You are now trusting in the Lord with all your heart so plan the weekly time with your family. The Lord will take care of the shortcomings.

Plan time with your family every week. This is when I will be home. Let them know your schedule. This way they can depend on you. If your schedule changes let them know. If there is going to be a big push let them know. But, by all means, spend quality time with them every single week. Be with them at church. This promotes continuity and peace in the heart of the whole family whether you have children or not. Just being married you and your spouse are a family.

Go out together in nature. Visit parks and recreations. Do stuff together. Make memories. These small seemingly insignificant things will make lifelong memories for them and for you. These are also opportunities to take mental photographs. When you are in the middle of a simple but beautiful moment do this: Look around, take in the surroundings and with a deep breath, close your eyes like the shutter of a camera and snap forever pictures. This photo will then develop in the mind to be stored for later. Then, later, in times of stress close your eyes and from the recesses of your mind pull out those moments and remember. This will decompress your emotions and put you back into a state of balance and well-being. These are the treasures that last forever, the treasures that no one can take from you.

Routine

Having a daily routine means not only that you are on track personally but that your family and friends can count on you when they need you. You might be saying to yourself, "Nobody needs me." If you are saying that the truth is that they need you but you are unreliable. They can't count on you because your schedule is all over the place or you are unreachable. Be someone that when the phone rings you pick it up and are happy to hear from whoever is calling. None of us are islands even if we are single and have no children. There are or will be people in your life that really need you. You are special because you have the ability to emotionally help those in your life in a way that others may not be able to. People will think, "We can count on you because you are predictable." This is a good thing.

Monthly meetings

Meetings in a certain spot in the home should be held once a month. These family gatherings are to give everyone the opportunity to catch up and know that they are all valued. There is always one in the group who likes to steal the attention so give them their time but then insist that everyone speak about what going on in their lives. This promotes purpose and healthy self-worth in the family unit. You also may need impromptu tribunal times. When two or more cannot agree then a mock trial with the parents as the judge and jury can take place.

Annual Landmarks

In my family growing up, we knew that every Thanksgiving we were going to my step-father's side of the family and every Christmas we were going to my Mom's side of the family. There was one of them that we all liked better than the other but the fact I learned later was that the continuity of knowing what was going to happen gave my little heart a settled peace. We hold dear, events that only happen once in a while and especially those that happen at the same time every year.

When my wife and I got married we talked about what we wanted as annual events in our lives. We continued some of the same traditions that we had growing up that were important to us. Christmas and Thanksgiving of course but she had one that I didn't know about. You see I was a Yankee and she was a southern bell. There were things I had yet to learn. The first big one was that just before the new year we had to go shopping for some special food. "What?" I exclaimed. "It's just New Year. Make a resolution and let's move on." "No!" She said. "We must have Black-eyed peas and cornbread or the new year will be a disaster." I didn't even know what a black-eyed pea was. But I soon found out how delicious her tradition was so it became a staple in our home.

Annual traditions are good. Create them for you and your family and pass them on. It creates a home environment that our children will always have good feelings about once they are gone and far from home. It could be another reason to keep them coming back home year after year. And, isn't that what we want?

Vacation Time

Early on in my sales career, I would always brag about how long it had been since I had a vacation. Everyone else was taking them as often as they could but I was selling more than they were so my thought was that the more time I put in the more money I would secure for my family. That was true up to a point. When I began to get overwhelmingly frustrated anger would settle in and I would yell and be, let's say, not myself with my family. I needed a vacation.

Taking vacations is important even if they are only a staycation. Wonderful things happen when the brain is allowed to relax for a week. Have you ever noticed that some of your best ideas come while you are either drifting off to sleep or just waking up in the morning? This is because your mind and body are no longer tensed from the day's work and are relaxed enough to allow for a positive flow of thought and creativity. Business owners and developers get some of their brightest ideas while on vacation.

This rejuvenation is a must or terrible things could happen at a young age. Without an extended downtime each year your body and mind could become so over-taxed that you just want to give up on the job. And, that could be at the point where you are just about to reach your highest potential. The worst thing to happen would be that your body just gives up entirely and disease sets in. Then all that you have worked so hard for is gone. VACATION TIME IS A LIFE BARRIER TO KEEPING YOU VIBRANT AND HEALTHY.

Although it is fun to plan and travel all over the nation and go places you have never been before wouldn't it be more relaxing to just plan a trip and spend more time there relaxing and enjoying each other's company and the scenery than always being on the road and having to stick to a constant time schedule. You do that every day all day long. Take a break. Find one or maybe two things at the most that everyone will enjoy and go do that. Pssst, and every other small vacation time just stay home and do nothing☺

There's a reason why The Lord after His work of creating the earth for us stopped and rested. It wasn't because He was tired. It was because we need Him all day, without work, one day every week. The word Sabbath means "To rest" Take the Sabbath off every week and watch how blessed your work, your family, and your relationship with the almighty will become.

13
CHAPTER

❖

Alone Time

As a growing top salesperson in the industry, you are hammered with phone calls, face-to-face meetings, accountabilities, goals, earthly bosses, stressful people, possible chargebacks, frustrating situations, and the list goes on. There are very important times that you have alone time with just you and the Lord.

Me and God

If the Devine Son of God couldn't handle His daily operations of helping others all by himself what makes us think that we can. All the time Jesus was found being alone with the heavenly Father in prayer. He was seeking His will. We should have that time every day, maybe in that special place where we go and talk with the heavenly Father just like Jesus did.

If The Lord knows the end from the beginning and knows what today will hold then He knows what paths to guide us in. He knows how to handle that angry customer or that earthly boss. I can tell Him all that hurts me or makes me happy. Yes, He knows but, He delights in us telling Him. He wants to hear from you more. Talk with Him in the morning. Walk with Him throughout the day. Listen to His answers when you are confused about what to do. Watch as He takes care of all your needs because you trust in Him.

In His Word

He did not leave us as orphans to try and figure this all out on our own. He not only loves us with everlasting love but cares for our small needs. As you read His love letter to us you will begin to see things that you may have never seen before. His promises are sure. He stands by them. His prophecies are true. He is always 100% accurate. His scriptures were written by Holy men of God that were moved by the Holy Spirit. 2 Peter 1:21 The words themselves are not perfect but the ideas are. He left it all in there. The good, the bad, and the ugly. That's how you know some dude didn't just sit down and start writing this. Because anybody that wants to make themselves look good would only put the good stuff in there. But, Wow! How much terrible stuff is in this message to us?

In the Holy Place of the Sanctuary, on the North side, was a table. On that table were two stacks of shew-bread. That bread represents several things for us today but one of the greatest things is His Holy Word. Jesus said, "I am the bread of Life". Two stacks symbolize both the old and the new testaments. None of them have been done away with only the ceremonial laws. Because Jesus was the fulfillment of those laws that pointed to Him. He then said to His disciples, "This is my body broken for you. Take and eat of it." We are to "digest" His Word daily so that we may live. Memorize parts of scripture and thereby fulfill His desire for you to "Hide it in your heart." "Write it on the tablet of your soul."

In His Presence

As His children, we are blessed. Not only are we blessed to be His children but we can live in His presence. The promise of the Messiah was amazing but something more amazing happened with the Messiah completed His mission on earth. He sent forth the promised power. The power of the Holy Spirit. Before this time the Spirit only dwelt among His people and would speak through His prophets. But in these last days, He lives in us. All who have been baptized by water and Spirit have now the Holy Spirit who lives within you.

There is therefore no humanly person that is any longer needed to reach the throne room of heaven where the almighty reigns. You can go to Him now and speak directly with Him by the power of the Holy Spirit that lives within you and by the blood of Jesus Christ who gave His blood for you. The High priest used to be the mediator for the people but since Jesus is the true High priest we can go directly to Him.

Tell it to others

We can't stay quiet for fear of ridicule. How many mighty people before us have spoken the truth boldly and even lost their lives for it? You know the numbers in sales. There are also numbers in telling others. How many do you need to tell to the number of how many will accept the truth. The fact is that there are so many people that are spiritually dying for the truths that you know and are learning. Become an instrument in the hands of The Lord, God, The Lord, The Almighty, and let Him change the lives of those you bring the truth to.

You may be in this position as a salesperson because this is where He needs you to reach certain people who could not be reached otherwise. Your heavenly appointed job is not to save the soul but to lead them to the water of life. There are those just waiting for someone to bring a small tidbit of truth to them to help them in their time of need and there you are. If you see someone searching do not hesitate to lead.

Another article in the Holy Place is the Candle Abrah. This candle abrah was filled with oil but only once it was perfectly hewn and ready. You are the Candlestick. You have gone through tough times to get to where you are with the Lord. Now, allow the Holy Spirit (Oil) to so fill your life that you light up the place with His power and glorify the Almighty for anyone willing to find Him to see Him.

I hope that your life becomes filled with blessings because you completely trust and rely on The Lord. Throughout anything that keeps you from giving Him your all. There is no room for two masters. Only Jesus. Let this be on your heart and mind. Only Jesus.

I am excited to see and hear your success stories as you become part of the top tier in sales mastery in this dark world. Let your light so shine that when all who see it will stand up and give thanks to the Lord for you. You are of great worth. Live it!

You are becoming a success. It is The Lord that is leading you there. Brag about Him to others. Let them know that He is the one that shows you things that you otherwise would not know. He doesn't just want to live forever with you in the hereafter but right now. His greatest desire is to live in your heart and mind. Become a new creation in Him and Praise Him with one success to another, as you become at top producer in you industry.

Printed in the United States
by Baker & Taylor Publisher Services